HOW TO BE
FILTHY
RICH

PRICELESS advice from the obscenely WEALTHY

Managing Editor: Simon Melhuish
Series Editor: Lee Linford
Design: Alan Shiner

Designed and compiled by
Mad Moose Press
for
Lagoon Books
PO Box 311, KT2 5QW, UK
PO Box 990676, Boston, MA 02199, USA

ISBN: 1-904139-25-6

www.madmoosepress.com
www.lagoongames.com

Printed in Hong Kong

HOW TO BE
FILTHY
RICH

PRICELESS advice from the obscenely WEALTHY

Easy money, dirty money, funny money. No matter how you see it - or how you make it - the reality is that we all need money to get by. But just how much do we really need? How much is enough?

Bill Gates, currently the world's richest individual, is worth around an estimated $53bn US dollars. An unimaginable sum, perhaps, but when put into greater perspective it's also a figure roughly equivalent to the annual GDP of Peru, Algeria or New Zealand and ten times that of Botswana or Nepal.

For those wondering just what it takes to become wealthier than a small - or even not so small - country, how to play the game and walk away stinking rich, who makes the rules and calls the shots and which path is most likely to be paved with gold, read on.

With quotes, quips and tips from the world's wealthiest, this really is money talking.

Richest of the rich
The wealthiest people on the planet:

1. Bill Gates   **US $52.8bn**

2. Warren E. Buffett   **US $35bn**

3. Karl & Theo Albrecht **US $26.8bn**

4. Paul G. Allen   **US $25.2bn**

5. Lawrence J. Ellison **US $23.5bn**

Source: www.forbes.com, 2002.

Don't be afraid to give up the good to go for the great.

John D. Rockefeller

If you can count your money, you don't have a billion dollars.

J. Paul Getty

After a certain point money is meaningless. It ceases to be the goal. The game is what counts.

Aristotle Onassis

Success is a lousy teacher. It seduces smart people into thinking they can't lose.

Bill Gates

Profile: **WILLIAM H. (BILL) GATES**

1955-
Estimated personal wealth: **US $52.8bn**

Computer programmer by the age of 13, Harvard dropout by 20, self-made billionaire by 31.

Gates is currently the world's richest individual. His vast fortune, which at its peak touched the $80bn mark, has burgeoned since the inception 'Micro-soft' in 1975.

From the early days, when Gates teamed up with school friend Paul Allen to provide a software solution for the world's first microcomputer, Microsoft have demonstrated expertise and business acumen in developing ideas and reworking existing innovations to create formidably successful products. MS-DOS, Windows and Internet Explorer are all prime examples.

Aggressive business tactics and avoiding the mistakes of competitors have enabled Microsoft to truly conquer global computing. When web browsers first emerged, Microsoft held back - for almost two years - yet Internet Explorer was soon established as the standard browser for the planet. Windows became the jewel in the Gates crown with over 85% of computers in the world now using the system. Such success ultimately led to various anti-trust battles with the US government regarding monopolistic activities. As a result Gates has taken a less prominent role in Microsoft.

The Gates fortune has been put to good use in many ways, including a $6bn dollar charitable donation - the largest bequest made by a living individual. Despite falls in Microsoft's stock price, Gates's interests in biotechnology and broadband communications will inevitably ensure his sustained wealth.

I like thinking big.
If you're going to be
thinking, you might as
well think big.

Donald Trump

A team effort is a lot of people doing what I say.

Michael Winner

If you see a bandwagon, it's too late.

Sir James Goldsmith

If I see something I like, I buy it; then I try to sell it.

Lord Grade

Surround yourself only with people who are going to lift you higher.

Oprah Winfrey

Where large sums of money are concerned, it is advisable to trust nobody.

Agatha Christie

If you don't drive your business, you will be driven out of business.

B. C. Forbes

Every day I get up and look through the Forbes list of the richest people in America. If I'm not there, I go to work.

Robert Orben

A rich man is one who isn't afraid to ask the salesman to show him something cheaper.

Anon

Ideas are a commodity.
Execution of them is not.

Michael Dell

Buy stocks like you buy your groceries, not like you buy your perfume.

Warren E. Buffett

Profile: **ARISTOTLE ONASSIS**

1906-1975
Estimated personal wealth: **US $3bn**

At the tender age of 17, Onassis fled Turkey for Argentina with little more than $60 in his pocket. Working as a telephone operator by night, he scraped together enough money to set about rebuilding the family tobacco business, which had been decimated during conflict between Greece and Turkey.

Once established, Onassis negotiated a trade agreement between Greece and Argentina enabling him to diversify into commodity import and export. By the age of 25 he was a millionaire.

During the infamous Depression of the 1930s Onassis sank his accumulated wealth into a fleet of cut-price freighters. Oil tankers, supertankers and whaling vessels were later acquired, creating one of the largest merchant shipping fleets in the world.

The tycoon's charm and hospitality drew the rich, famous and powerful alike. All were lavishly entertained at parties aboard his luxurious yacht, the 'Christina O' - Frank Sinatra, Marilyn Monroe, Winston Churchill and JFK to name but a few. The yacht also provided the setting for the wedding reception of Prince Rainier and Princess Grace.

Onassis made a less successful move into the airline business in the 1950s, running Olympic, the Greek national airline. His controversial private life, including his 'friendship' with opera singer Maria Callas, and dubious business activities - whaling included - stirred up both interest and criticism.

I have no friends and no enemies - only competitors.

Aristotle Onassis

Spare no expense to make everything as economical as possible.

Samuel Goldwyn

Why pay a dollar for a bookmark? Why not use the dollar for a bookmark?

Steven Spielberg

If you can run one business well, you can run any business well.

Sir Richard Branson

If you pay peanuts, you get monkeys.

Sir James Goldsmith

Studying economics
is not a good preparation
for dealing with it.

George Soros

Give me the luxuries of life and I will willingly do without the necessities.

Frank Lloyd Wright

I'm tired of hearing about money, money, money, money, money. I just want to play the game, drink Pepsi, wear Reebok.

Shaquille O'Neal

Time is the scarcest resource and unless it is managed nothing else can be managed.

Peter F. Drucker

It is observed that successful people get ahead in the time that other people waste.

Henry Ford

I know of nothing more despicable and pathetic than a man who devotes all the hours of the waking day to the making of money for money's sake.

John D. Rockefeller

You reach a point where you don't work for money.

Walt Disney

Risk comes from not knowing what you're doing.

Warren E. Buffett

Everything in life is luck.

Donald Trump

If the boy and girl walk off into the sunset hand-in-hand in the last scene, it adds ten million to the box office.

George Lucas

Profile: **GEORGE LUCAS**

1944-
Estimated personal wealth: **US $3bn**

The name George Lucas is synonymous with Star Wars, the box-office blockbuster written and directed by Lucas and released in 1977. The movie grossed in excess of $400m, but the deal struck by Lucas with Universal Studios saw his earnings predominantly accumulating from spin-off merchandise and sequel movies.

However, it was an earlier award-winning movie, American Graffiti, that first lined the cinematographer's pockets with millions of dollars. For every dollar spent on American Graffiti, Lucas saw an astounding fifty dollar return. Such profit financed the director's ultimate dream, Star Wars, first conceived whilst he recuperated in hospital following an amateur motor racing accident that nearly cost his teenage life.

Lucas's concept of The Force changed the face of the film industry. Technologically, he wanted the impossible. And to achieve the impossible he created a pioneering special effects company, Industrial Light and Magic. ILM later went on to develop the Jurassic Park dinosaurs and THX cinema sound (its name derived from an earlier, less successful collaboration with Francis Ford Coppola on the movie THX1138).

Lucasfilm and ILM aside, the writer/producer/director has also established LucasArts - one of the first companies to release games on CD ROM - and the George Lucas Educational Foundation which employs technology with a view to making learning fun. More recently George Lucas has embarked on his second Star Wars trilogy - the prequel to the legendary original.

Every few seconds it changes - up an eighth, down an eighth - it's like playing a slot machine. I lose $20 million, I gain $20 million...

Ted Turner

Time is money.

Sir James Goldsmith

Formula for success: Rise early, work hard, strike oil.

J. Paul Getty

I don't want to make money. I just want to be wonderful.

Marilyn Monroe

Gentlemen prefer bonds.

Andrew Mellon

Education costs money, but then so does ignorance

Claus Moser

There are people who have money and people who are rich.

Coco Chanel

Money is like an arm or a leg - use it or lose it.

Henry Ford

Profile: **HENRY FORD**

1863 - 1947
Estimated personal wealth **US $1bn**

Ford's dream was to produce a gasoline powered vehicle, affordable to the middle class.

His interest in mechanics soon drew him away from the family farm, moving to industrial Detroit where he initially worked on steam engines and later came under the employ of Thomas Edison. Ford constructed his first car, the Quadricycle, in his spare time and by 1903 he had established The Ford Motor Car Company.

Ford devised the assembly line, revolutionizing automobile manufacture in process. The mass produced Ford Model T arrived in 1908, production reaching a staggering 15 million units - around half the world's entire automobile output - by the time it ceased in 1927.

Ford spread the rewards. Workers were paid more than double the industry standard wage, but conditions were attached; smoking was banned, gambling and alcohol discouraged. The high wage was also intended to compensate for the monotony of assembly line work.

Ford invested heavily, buying up everything from iron ore mines to ships, thus ensuring self sufficiency from source to market. The vast River Rouge Plant was built to cover all aspects of automobile production from ore refining and glass manufacture to parts forging and vehicle assembly. Nearly 100,000 men were employed company-wide and such resources proved invaluable in handling aircraft, jeep and tank production during WWII.

With time, Ford's singular vision allowed competitors, such as GM, to gain ground. Ford detested unions and began to treat workers like machines. He saw little reason to offer consumers choice. GM embraced both. Such factors coupled with Ford's openly public anti-Semitic views seriously damaged the company, and it was Henry Ford II who eventually took on the task of restoring the Ford reputation. Henry Ford's personal wealth would equate to somewhere in the region of US$36bn today.

Failure is inevitable. Success is elusive.

Steven Spielberg

If you think you're too small to have an impact, try going to bed with a mosquito.

Anita Roddick

There are two fools in this world. One is the millionaire who thinks that by hoarding money he can somehow accumulate real power, and the other is the penniless reformer who thinks that if only he can take the money from one class and give it to another, all the world's ills will be cured.

Henry Ford

The best way to help the poor is not to become one of them.

Laing Hancock

Keep looking tanned, live in an elegant building (even if you're in the cellar), be seen in smart restaurants (even if you nurse one drink), and if you borrow, borrow big.

Aristotle Onassis

Lead, follow, or get out of the way.

Ted Turner

In this business, by the time you realize you're in trouble, it's too late to save yourself. Unless you're running scared all the time, you're gone.

Bill Gates

What you do is begin as a billionaire. Then you go into the airline business.

Sir Richard Branson

(advice on how to become a millionaire)

The most expensive habit in the world is celluloid, not heroin, and I need a fix every few years.

Steven Spielberg

Profile: **JEAN PAUL GETTY**

1892-1976
Estimated personal wealth: **US $3bn**

Getty's billions were extracted from oil, a business that captured his imagination whilst working as a casual laborer on his father's rigs.

Upon completing his education, Getty sought financial support in order to establish his own independent oil company. The high-risk, high-stakes nature of oil exploration was a big attraction for a man who thrived on taking gambles. Within two years, and aged just 23, he'd struck oil in a big way, notching up his first US$1m in the process.

During the 1930s Depression, Getty ploughed his financial reserves into oil company stocks which were changing hands at rock-bottom prices. His vision was to build an oil empire - not an easy task. Full acquisition of Tidewater Oil Co., for example, resulted in a mammoth 19 year-long battle and required a complex network of holding companies to mask the tycoon's involvement.

In time, Getty built the all-encompassing independent oil business he had dreamt of. It incorporated a broad portfolio of companies handling exploration, drilling, refining, transportation and sales. Acquisitions, re-organization and mergers led to the formation of the Getty Oil Company, of which its namesake remained president - and very much in control - until he died in 1976.

Getty became one of the richest men in the world. Much of his fortune was reaped from risky dealings in the Middle East where the discovery of vast oil deposits propelled his wealth into the billions. Getty was a recluse and an eccentric, renowned for both his extravagances and miserly ways. His turbulent private life, entailing five failed marriages and the high-profile kidnapping of his grandson, ensured persistent media attention and public curiosity.

No one can possibly achieve any real or lasting success or 'get rich' in business by being a conformist.

J. Paul Getty

The more you get, the more you get.

Tom Petty

Making money is fun, but it's pointless if you don't use the power it brings.

John Bentley

Wall Street is the only place people ride in a Rolls-Royce to get advice from people who take the subway.

Warren E. Buffett

Sometimes your best investments are the ones you don't make.

Donald Trump

What am I supposed to do with the money I earn? Give it back?

Rod Stewart

Being good is good business.

Anita Roddick

I defy anyone who's ever done a deal with Bob Maxwell to say he didn't get a full 12 annas for his rupee.

Robert Maxwell

(NB: there are 16 annas to 1 rupee)

If you've got a mind-shattering talent, you want a million dollars for it.

Elton John

Somebody said to me, "But the Beatles were anti-materialistic." That's a huge myth. John and I literally used to sit down and say, "Now, let's write a swimming pool."

Paul McCartney

Profile: (KEITH) RUPERT MURDOCH

1931-
Estimated personal wealth **US $5.7bn**

Since leaving his native Australia and acquiring US citizenship, Murdoch has steadily assembled a vast global media conglomerate encompassing television, film, publishing and the internet. Entering the media world with a small, ailing local Australian newspaper, inherited from his father, the tycoon's assets now include 20th Century Fox, BSkyB, Star TV, The New York Post, The Times, HarperCollins and the LA Dodgers, among others. His attempts so far to buy Manchester United Football Club have, however, failed.

Murdoch's willingness to embrace change and employ cutting-edge technology, coupled with his ambitions to control both media content and distribution have been his making. Success has brought with it controversy and Murdoch's business tactics - including political influence and monopolistic practices - have drawn considerable criticism. But criticism is not something that Rupert Murdoch generally chooses to acknowledge.

Wealth and power aside, the billionaire has accumulated more than his fair share of admirers and enemies alike. He has been accused of being an unpredictable tyrant, a loner, a ruthless predator and a control freak who refuses to delegate responsibility. But, despite a few glitches, he has undeniably achieved enormous success.

Now into his seventies there is growing speculation that Murdoch's eldest son, Lachlan, will take the helm of the tycoon's empire. It has also been suggested that, without Murdoch, the News Corporation could cease to exist, for few - if any - have been allowed to acquire a complete understanding of the infinitely complex business in its entirety.

The buck stops with the guy who signs the checks.

Rupert Murdoch

The man who does not work for the love of work but only for money is not likely to make money nor find much fun in life.

Charles M. Schwab

I had no ambition to
make a fortune.
Mere money-making
has never been my goal.
I had an ambition to build.

John D. Rockefeller

If someone as blessed as I am is not willing to clean out the barn, who will?

H. Ross Perot

Part of the $10 million I spent on gambling, part on booze and part on women. The rest I spent foolishly.

George Raft

I buy when other people are selling.

J. Paul Getty

Money is an article which may be used as a universal passport to everywhere except Heaven, and as a universal provider of everything but happiness.

Wall Street Journal

Whoever said money can't buy happiness simply didn't know where to go shopping.

Bo Derek

A friendship founded on business is better than a business founded on friendship.

John D. Rockefeller

Everyone wants to ride with you in the limo, but what you need is someone who will take the bus with you when the limo breaks down.

Oprah Winfrey

If you start a company from scratch, and you don't have any financial backing, the only thing that matters is survival.

Sir Richard Branson

Profile: **SIR RICHARD BRANSON**

1950-
Estimated personal wealth **US $1.4bn**

Self-made billionaire, entrepreneurial genius, people's hero and the flamboyant public face of the Virgin global empire.

Branson's beginnings were truly small, selling advertising space from a public call box for a student magazine that he started as a teenager. Virgin Music rapidly followed, selling cut price records to students by mail order, initially utilizing the magazine as a sales medium. Branson went on to set up the highly successful Virgin Records - a record label that would become one of the industry's big players - signing acts including Mike Oldfield, The Rolling Stones, Peter Gabriel and Culture Club. The sale of his beloved record label in 1992 raised around US $1bn - vital capital injected into Virgin Atlantic.

Today, the Virgin Group comprises more than 200 companies operating in profoundly diverse markets; music, airlines, travel, finance, weddings, cola, publishing, car sales, commercial radio, mobile phones and energy included.

Richard Branson's media magnetism largely stems from his outrageous publicity stunts and an appetite for taking on huge corporate conglomerates in their established markets - most notably British Airways and Coca Cola - and making a significant impact. Virgin Atlantic, for example, began life as a single leased aircraft operating between London and New York.

The Virgin name has become a powerful global brand, synonymous with its creator and built on an ethos of fun, approachability and audacity. Calculated risks that many would consider to be lunacy have netted Branson a tidy fortune. However, one or two more recent ventures have proved exceptionally tough, most notably his involvement with British rail travel.

A criminal is a person with predatory instincts who has not sufficient capital to form a corporation.

Howard Scott

Once you consent to some concession, you can never cancel it and put things back the way they are.

Howard Hughes

The meek shall inherit the earth, but not the mineral rights.

J. Paul Getty

Money is like manure. If you spread it around it does a lot of good, but if you pile it up in one place it stinks like hell.

Clint Murchison

If women didn't exist, all the money in the world would have no meaning.

Aristotle Onassis

Entrepreneurs are risk-takers, willing to roll the dice with their money or reputation on the line in support of an idea or enterprise. They willingly assume responsibility for the success or failure of a venture and are answerable for all its facets. The buck not only stops at their desks, it starts their too.

Victor Kiam

All boats rise in high tide.

Warren E. Buffett

for even more insightful

advice, check out

'How to be a Huge Success',

also available from

Mad Moose Press.